PURE
The Devotional

REASSIGNING THE PURPOSE OF YOUR
EYES, HEART & HANDS

Allen K. Hunter

ZA'VAN GAIL PUBLISHING

SEATTLE, WASHINGTON

PUCK

Scripture quotations taken from the Amplified® Bible (AMP),
Copyright © 2015 by The Lockman Foundation
Used by permission. www.Lockman.org

Scripture taken from the Modern English Version. Copyright © 2014 by Military Bible Association. Used by permission. All rights reserved.

All Scripture marked with the designation "GW" is taken from *GOD'S WORD®*.
© 1995, 2003, 2013, 2014, 2019, 2020 by God's Word to the Nations Mission Society. Used by permission.

All Scripture taken from the New Century Version®. Copyright © 2005 by Thomas Nelson. Used by permission. All rights reserved.

Allen K. Hunter/Za'Van Gail Publishing
www.AllenKHunter.com

Ordering Information:
Contact PastorAllen@DominionAndPowerMinistries.com

PURE: The Devotional/ Allen K. Hunter. —1st ed.
ISBN 978-0-9970441-4-0

i

Contents

Dedication

I dedicate this book to my granny. You always believed in me, even when it didn't look promising. Your encouragement brought me so much joy. You told me you wanted me to grow up to be a fine, noble man and that you wanted me to do great things. Well granny, I've done just that! I'm doing great things. I hope you're proud of me! I love and miss you so much! Oh, by the way I married an intelligent woman who graduated from PV, I know you would like her, hahaha. Continue to Rest in Peace Ernestine Outly, my Granny.

I also would like to dedicate this devotional to all that are struggling with being pure. This book was written especially for you. I want to give you hope! IT'S NEVER TOO LATE! If God can change me, he can change you. He loves you just the way you are, he just wants better for you. I want you to know you're not alone; I'm here for you, along with others. You can always contact me; my email is on the back of this book. Reach out to me when you need someone that won't judge you. Love you and may Gods peace be with you.

Your Friend - Pornographer to Pastor,

Allen K. Hunter

Acknowledgements

I want to thank the Holy Spirit for giving me the power, authority, freedom, insight, and words to pen this devotional. To my Lord and Savior Jesus The Christ, thank you for loving me through my mess. I appreciate you for dying on the cross for my sins, making away to have communication with our God. Thank you, God, for choosing and ordaining me. I never knew I could be so great because of you. One last thing, thank you for thinking enough of me to send your Son here on earth as an example of how to live and use the power you have given us as your children.

To my daughter, Kayson Alex Hunter, we haven't seen each other in 4yrs, and I know God is working it out for us to reunite, a matter of fact it's already worked out. We just have to be patient and that has been one of the most difficult challenges for me my Sweet Pea. Kayson wherever you are, if you're reading this, just know DADDY LOVES YOU SOOOOOO MUCH, and I can't wait to see and hold you, and buy you whatever you want, lol – **The tables are turning....**

My God, to my parents Pastor D.E.C. & Artricia Matthews, I thank God for the reconnection, the rekindling of our relationship. You guys have been through so much as Pastors *(I'm a living witness)* I've seen the struggles, the grind, the excellence, The Pain and the building of. I've learned so much from the both of you, you all truly have a heart for gods people. With all the discipline *(whooping's and grounding, lol)* I must say you have raised a fine and nobleman (in my granny's voice). I TRULY DO LOVE YOU GUYS! – **It Isn't Over**

To my immediate family, Vanessa Taylor (Gran), Zasmyne (the most intellectual daughter), Cousin Theo (Mr. Wealthy) Cousin Derek (Preacher in the making). You guys rock! I love our family prayer calls every week, it's so encouraging to see the growth. – *Trip To The Maldives, On Me*

To my PNW family, especially The City of Seattle. I genuinely do love my city and the people that make it up. God is with us. God has so much stored for our city. WE ARE THE NEW AZUZA! – *Here Comes The Revival*

Now to the most important person other than God, my Wife, Lady Jay. Woman of God, I do value you so much. You push me to be better; you hold me accountable; you love me unconditionally. You walk in integrity; you are most definitely a virtuous woman God used you to push me to do what I thought I would never or could do, write a devotional book. Jacelyn, you've taught me how to study, pray, speak, walk in my authority. You are my personal Prophet. I'm so honored for us to be able to do ministry together. We are changing lives, communities; now let's shift THE WORLD with the help of the Holy Ghost. LOVE YOU WITH ALL MY HEART! (You're 5'5) – *You're Stuck With Me For Life, Even When We Get To Heaven, hahaha*

Endorsement

Freedom. Say it again out loud. FREEDOM! In his book, "Pure – Reassigning the Purpose of Your Eyes, Heart, and Hands" Pastor Allen Hunter facilitates a very personal, emotional, and spiritual journey to FREEDOM for anyone with the boldness to confront head on the chains of sexual addiction. Pastor Allen unflinchingly shares his personal testimony from captivity to liberty in his own life, as he guides the reader to extreme honesty in how to achieve victory and true freedom. Say it again out loud. FREEDOM!

I recently met Pastor Allen Hunter and from my first encounter with him, I felt right away he possesses a rare and refreshing authenticity. After spending some time with him and reading his book, "Pure," my hunch was confirmed. Here he tackles the issue of sexual addiction with a multi-pronged strategy of transparency, vulnerability, honesty, scripture, prayer, deliverance and accountability. Nothing hidden. The strategy to disempower and defeat this monster is galvanized in his approach to expose without shame, to confront with love, incorporating a biblical perspective, and to journey together through relationship and community to a glorious life of freedom. Take this journey with Pastor Allen. Come out of the shadows of shame! Embrace the power of heaven's true love and freedom! Find here the peace and satisfaction of the pure life! Those who have taken this journey will tell you unequivocally you will not regret it!

Michael Proctor

Foreword

We were married just after six months of meeting and soon we will have been married 4 years this year. I can honestly say I am so proud of you and even that is an understatement. To be able to write the foreword for your first book is beyond an honor. I have seen firsthand how you have fought through your own spiritual, mental and emotional battle within yourself to consider yourself qualified and equipped enough to even tell the story that you are so honestly telling throughout these pages. God has ordained you to be the open book that you are.

I applaud you boldly and while standing next to you screaming the loudest from within the crowd or the audience of just me and The Holy Trinity! The pure devotional is going to absolutely change lives because your life has been changed. You've allowed God to do such an amazing work in you, and our intimacy, relationship and friendship is so very blessed because of it! I absolutely love you!

Keep walking with God. He has you. He's for you. He loves you. He has affirmed you. This is your destiny Allen K Hunter producer, now author.

Lovingly & Always Your Wife,
Jacelyn "Lady Jay" Hunter

Prelude

I want to ask you a vital question. In our sex-saturated culture, how can one strive to live a pure life? You may be thinking, is there even such a thing. Others may then ask what does pure mean anyway. Because the truth is, no one is pure because no one can be perfect, right?

Within this devotional, we will discuss the crucial involvement of the heart, eyes, and hands have in living what God has spoken to my heart, which is a *pure* lifestyle. Our heart, eyes, and hands have such a big responsibility in the way we live. Their importance from this day forward you will learn can *never* be underestimated.

I will ask that you do not allow the word *PURE* to intimidate you. This word, for some, tends to boast a type of perfection. The definition of *pure* that I desire for you to rest upon in regard to this devotional is; *free of any contamination, wholesome, and untainted by immorality, especially* that of a sexual nature. *In Greek, pure is defined as "Katharos," moral or ethically free from corrupt desire, sin, and guilt, which* is not at all about perfection **but one's commitment to a lifestyle.** But first, allow me to introduce my story so you can begin to embrace the journey you and I are going to take.

Hello. My name is Allen K. Hunter, and I was addicted to pornography and masturbation for most of my 41 years. I have been truly set free since 2018 **(recent, huh? *I didn't want to be a hypocrite as I was writing this),* and it wasn't easy. But I wouldn't settle for not being free, and the refusal of anything less is why I can write this devotional. Come, let's go.

MY TRANSPARENT MOMENT

From the tender age of 5 to the adulthood age of 39, I wasn't thinking about being *pure*. I certainly would not have known what it even meant. Age 5 is where my experience of being tainted by molestation, corrupted by porn and influenced to masturbate began. I will tell you that something that started at the age of 5 for me was the something I would go on to do four to seven times a day; I would spend hours upon hours being entangled in the "web of porn" searching for images and videos of what pleased me. Click by click; I began experiencing new fetishes that I didn't know I would like. They were strange. They included a strong attraction to feet and went on to morph into what I craved, which was porn type sexual encounters. It had me so wrapped up. It was as if I was married to this addiction! I cannot lie. I enjoyed how the women looked at me through the television or computer as if they were there with and just for me. It was "the wow factor" for me because they were acknowledging me. I enjoyed the provocative way they would dress along with the high heels, which made their legs look even more attractive to me.

There was a part of me that knew, in reality, these women were just actresses, but I ignored that fact and continued to fall in love deeper and deeper. All I knew is that they knew what I liked. In my mind, I had an ongoing relationship with them. I could be with them in the comfort of my own space whenever I wanted; however, I wanted and could get them to do whatever I wanted over and over again. It was like I was in control; I wasn't worried about the women liking me or not liking me because of how I looked or my financial status. There was no judgment. I did not have to measure up. In my mind, these encounters were real. And in my mind, I did not have to face a fear that often dealt with me regarding getting an STD. STD meant pain, and I didn't like pain. This was yet another reason why the tie to this addiction was so strong because it made me feel safe. After all, these encounters allowed me to practice "safe sex." With that worry out of the way, I fell in love even more with the way impurity made me feel as it invited me to each experience, which caused me to keep craving more as I chased those imprinted images.

THE IMPORTANCE OF PURITY

Purity was the last thing on my mind. I had no concept of it. Until I learned why purity was necessary; and why my eyes, hands, and heart had to be re-assigned to my purpose and not in bondage to the insatiable appetite of what I liked them to do.

I wasn't using my hands for either shielding or attacking; being pure with my hands wasn't the focal point, satisfying the flesh was. I didn't know how to. I wasn't using my eyes for visions of greatness or preparation. I didn't know how to. I wanted to see more perversion. My heart couldn't properly love because I didn't know love without pornography. Once again, I will say, "I didn't know how to."

Then I began to learn about the fact that I needed something. That something was *purity*. Purity benefits you and me in several ways. Don't underestimate purity's power in your life, or the damaging consequences its opposite *impurity* can cause. The most meaningful benefit of "purity" is righteousness. Righteousness allows you access into God's holy presence, where bondages can be broken and a place where restoration can occur. You and I cannot afford to have revoked access to the presence of God.

> **Matthew 5:8 AMP** Jesus said, "Blessed [anticipating God's presence, spiritually mature] are the pure in heart [those with integrity, moral courage, and godly character], for they will see God.

The heart is exceptionally significant because, in the Bible, the heart stands for the seat, source, and organizer of our thoughts, attitudes, desires, personality, and motivation. It is equal with our modern use of "mind". The mind is where we hold knowledge, feelings, motivations, affections, desires, likes, and dislikes. Like the heart, the mind is not just about remembering. It is a sensory memory bank.

The heart is central and is the message of this beatitude. Proverbs 4:23 reads, ***"Keep your heart with all diligence, for out of it spring the issues of life".*** Once we have received Jesus Christ as our Lord and Savior, we meet with our initial cleansing, purifying our hearts. Then the development of sanctification initiates as we go on to arrive at perfection. Not perfection as in *flawless*, but perfection as in *maturity*.

Sanctification does not all take place in an instant. It is a process, and as we have all discovered from Scripture and our own experience since baptism, human nature is still very much alive within us, read Romans 7:13-25. Apostle Paul also confirms this in *Galatians 5:17, "For the flesh lusts against the Spirit, and the Spirit against the flesh; and these are contrary to one another so that you cannot do the things that you wish."* – ***You will always have a battle while living on earth.***

I need your intentionality about giving your full attention to what purity also promotes: caution, discernment, and good choices while stopping corruption in thought, word, and action. Purity supports good health, long life, leads to satisfaction and peace. Purity assists you in being accountable in your life and pulls you toward godliness, honoring the conscience God gave you. It warns you of potholes and helps you live free of guilt and regret *(we all need that help)*. Having a pure lifestyle aids you in developing a community of loving people with honor and affection. It manages your relationships with others and enables you to provide an example for them to follow, ***BE A TRENDSETTER!***

One last word of advice before we jump into this devotional further, purity is obtainable for you. *Yes, for you!* It is possible to reassign what your hands, eyes, and heart responds to doing. You can overcome the urges that tend to trap you.

The journey you are about to take through this devotional will have a profound impact on your life. It will break the bondage of sexual addictions, hate, low self-esteem, the impossible will become the miraculous, improvement of the character will occur, and a sound mind will manifest. Your God-given power and authority will be activated. You will experience the "Chain Breaker" that is truth and confrontation in Christ Jesus.

Purifying your heart, eyes, and hands will show in your thoughts, words, choices, attitudes, relationships, etc. ARE YOU READY FOR YOUR JOURNEY? LET'S GO!!!

> ***2 Corinthians 6:7 AMP -*** *teaches us, "in [speaking] the word of truth, in the power of God; by the weapons of righteousness for the right hand [like holding the sword to attack] and for the left [like holding the shield to defend]."*

Guilty Hands

Masturbation was my vice, and it was personal for me. I enjoyed the experience of it, how it made me feel, and mostly how safe it was. And because of the satisfaction of those feelings, it became a daily routine for me. I was intimate with masturbation, and it unapologetically became my addiction.
-Allen K. Hunter

Have you ever liked an activity so much that it became a part of you and changed how you operated? Did it become an escape for you? Masturbation became that for me, along with becoming a part of me. But first, so that you can fully understand, I must take you back to the beginning of how masturbation got underneath my skin. You need to know that my addiction to masturbation manifested out of the trauma of me being molested, which was carried out by close friends of my family at the time. Yes, it happened more than one time, and by more than one person. The life of my addiction was also birthed through my friends as they began to let me in on their sexual experiences. This encounter I must share with you.

One day my friends and I were playing outside. I was around six years old at the time. As the day went on, we happened to meet up with an older male friend in the neighborhood whose name was Peter. We continued to play and include

Peter in our game. After some time, the playing stopped, and the conversation began to change. Peter started talking about a sexual experience he recently had with a girl. My friends and I were all ears! Peter was, fortunately, but unfortunately for the child-me very detailed! And I will tell you that those *details* followed me far beyond that moment.

He described the release he experienced after being with a woman and how euphoric it felt. Peter said, "As I released, it went everywhere! It felt so good!" Peter described vividly how his emission went everywhere. He made sounds familiar with cartoons in my six-year-old mind at the time. Was Peter describing an erupting volcano? Would I erupt? I honestly did not know. But I became curious, excited, and wanted to experience that euphoria for myself. But with whom I remember thinking at the age of six. Before I could answer that question fully, I became consumed with merely *having the experience.* Peter proceeded to tell us about his sexual adventures as his descriptions became visual. Weeks later, Peter brought us some Playboy Magazines, which then rocked my little world even more and opened the door of porn.

I stated before that I did not know whom I would have those sexual encounters with that Peter described. I did not have much self-esteem. While growing up, *I was told I was ugly, fat and that girls wouldn't want me— and those words sunk deep within my identity before it could even be established.* As I grew, those words would latch onto my manhood as it struggled to develop. The unsatisfiable hunger to masturbate was fueled by the hurt, pain, the rejection I felt daily, shame, and loneliness. So, for years to come, masturbation and my private enjoyment of pornography was my safe place. It was a place I did not have to be concerned with the embarrassment I felt about my image or the fear of being rejected by women. I didn't have to work hard in my safe place.

THE EXPERIENCE

> *Do not offer the parts of your body to serve sin, as things to be used in doing evil. Instead, offer yourselves to God as people who have died and now live. Offer the parts of your body to God to be used in doing good – **Romans 6:13 (MEV)***

This scripture references the use of our body parts to satisfy impure desires. Impure is defined as being morally wrong, especially when it concerns sexual matters. The penis, vagina, hands, breasts, feet, lips, tongue, buttock, and non-sexual things can arouse our minds as we can imagine touching, feeling, or seeing them. When illicit thoughts develop around body parts, it becomes easy for one to be persuaded in using them to engage in impure acts. Thoughts entice and seduce. It starts with one and then builds a large file of illicit thoughts to pull from.

As time went on, I knew I wanted deliverance. I took steps to get closer to Jesus. God began to tug at my spiritual ear so I could hear Him tell me that my hands were meant for more than masturbation. I had an incredible experience with Him that changed how I saw my hands. I began to study the word while sitting in His presence as I learned what my hands we created for. Then God gave me the following scriptures, and this is what they taught me.

> ***Job 17:9 (MEV)*** *But those who do right will continue to do right, and those whose hands are not dirty with sin will grow stronger.*

Weightless hands are easier to use to praise God, the Creator.

> **Mark 16:18 (Jesus Speaks)** they shall lay hands on the sick, and they shall recover.

Your hands where created to heal God's people.

> **2 Corinthians 6:7 (AMP)** by the weapons of righteousness for the right hand [like holding the sword to attack] and for the left [like holding the shield to defend].

Your hands where created to defend nations.

> **Psalm 132:4 (God's Word Translation)** Lift your hands toward the holy place and praise the Lord.

Your hands where created to worship God and God only.

So, my hands needed to be pure because they were created to defend, attack when necessary, heal, praise, and worship God, The Creator. I honestly did not know the use of my hands mattered so much. No awareness was afforded to me that shined a light so brightly that my hands carried such a mighty purpose. Without this powerful purpose known to me is why I had always thought of my hands as ***guilty hands***. My hands had been heavy with guilt. Maybe you feel the weight of guilt sitting in the palm of your hands right now due to what you've done or what you are thinking about doing. Guilt always comes after the satisfaction of pleasure when performing an act your conscious knows isn't right.

I remember crying to God out of guilt on many occasions, verbally declaring, "I don't want to do this anymore! I'm sick and tired of this!" But was my cry for help sincere? I kept masturbating. I kept looking at porn. I then developed new desires that I would later learn were fetishes. My addiction wanted to try new things as it had me going places that I had no business going. I was doing activities I vowed I would never do, becoming even more ashamed, feeling more stupid, beyond useless, and drained! But I continued to say, *"I AINT GONNA DO IT AGAIN"!*

I thought every cry for help was the last time. Until I realized pleasure was only present during the act. Guilt was there afterward. The cycle is deceptively vicious. After *the feel-good fades away, guilt will come.* Does this pleasure, then guilt, back, and forth inner fight sound familiar?

Know this: The love of sin will always cause you to endure and accept the shame it brings. The strength of my addiction, the safety I felt, and the low self- esteem kept driving me and pulling on me to keep going and do what I knew was wrong, even before I turned over my life entirely to Jesus. So, know that before a person secures salvation, conviction is possible. If you have not received Jesus Christ as your Lord and Savior, conviction is still possible. How? God has written the Ten Commandments on every human living being's heart, and when one of those commandments is violated, the heart beings to speak.

I believe that if you are reading this devotional, you're sick and tired of the impure activities that you are doing with your hands. It's like you want to help it, but can't help it, while at the same time you're attracted to it. This bondage is causing you frustration in your life as the guilt intensifies. I also believe something on the inside of you wants to do what is right with your hands as you submit them to their assigned purpose. This journey can be challenging. But know a successful journey for you is possible. You are not alone.

Your healing begins with confrontation. God is standing with you. Let Him speak to your heart as He begins to help you with assigning your hands purpose, integrity, peace, and His power.

LET'S PRAY

I don't want to lead you in a word for word prayer. I want you to pray from your heart, and mean it! Declare what you need and how you are going to change it. Remember, being truthful and transparent with yourself is what brings freedom to your life. Don't be embarrassed; it's just you and God. *You will overcome by the words out of your mouth, Revelation 12:11 –* YOU GOT THIS, IN JESUS NAME.

RECAP "GUILTY HANDS"

What purpose were your hands assigned to?

- Praise God, The Creator
- To Heal God's People
- To Defend Nations
- Worship God and God Only

REFLECTION

Discuss with God what purpose specifically that He has assigned to YOUR hands as it relates to YOUR purpose?

Journal

_____

_____

_____

_____

_____

_____

_____

_____

_____

_____

_____

_____

_____

The Heart Has Thoughts

We all have things we treasure; it might be prize objects, activities, experiences, or memories. And what we most value is what is vital to our hearts.
-Allen K. Hunter

Back in the "Guilty Hands" section of this devotional, I told you about my encounter growing up as a kid and my first experience with an adult magazine. That moment created continuous emotional stimulation coupled with memories of which captivated my mind 24-7. Instead of being able to dream of greatness, I imagined my gratifying picture for my next private session. Those images never quit appearing. By the time I was seven, I would always think about the women I had seen in that first magazine Peter had given me. The fantasies of how she would feel and how I could, in my mind, make her like me resumed. My heart wanted her attention; my body wanted her responsiveness. It was on my mind all day, every day! It undeniably had my commitment. My drums were the only thing that could sneak in and momentarily distract my catalog of images from running through my mind because they at least still had some of my heart on reserve. Provocative images and pictures ran me.

A PROBLEM I DID NOT SEE COMING

Lust wanted yet more of me. At the age of 18, my problem began to escalate to another level; as I adopted a more profound fetish. But I knew that to satisfy the craving for my new-found obsession, I had to take sex out of my mind and bring it into my reality. I then began to date, and just like in my fantasies, the women I chose in real life were beautiful. However, unlike my imagination, the women were not eager to please. They used me, mistreated me, and made it crystal clear they did not love me. My esteem at the time was not able to handle my make-believe life, not matching my reality. This reality ship-wrecked any resemblance I had of confidence. Time progressed with little improvement in my esteem.

At the age of 22, I got married for the first time. This marriage was verbally and emotionally abusive to me. Smack-talking was a massive part of how she communicated with me. The mouthing off, I hated it. The smart-talking, I hated it. Me having to beg for sex, I hated it.

At the age of 30, I got married for the 2nd time, and it was boring, no excitement. We would have sex only two times a month. It was an act of God to have sex three times a month. Even in this marriage, I had to initiate it. It was as if she was not attracted to me! I HATED THAT!

At the age of 34, I got married for the 3rd time and still looking for the love, I desperately wanted and needed. She always had something smart to say, never appreciative, never considered my feelings, and guess what, I had to beg for sex in this marriage. But unlike the other two marriages, she encouraged me to abandon my attempt at freedom from porn and masturbate. I was encouraged to keep doing it. I COULD NOT TAKE IT AND DID NOT FULLY UNDERSTAND IT! What was wrong with me? **Can you recognize a trend?**

As some of the most influential women I married abused me verbally and emotionally, feelings of emasculation deepened without my knowing it. My manhood was severely fractured. Subsequently, another problem was brewing that I did not see coming.

At the age of 40, I got married for the 4th time to my current and final wife, Jacelyn, aka "Lady Jay." It was a rocky road for both of us when we first got married. This is only a story my wife can tell. Babe, take it away.

I just remember Allen being so abrasive when I would not agree with him in the beginning of our marriage. During those times of disagreement, he would become insulting and go for the jugular to make his point. It was as I was his enemy. Allen would make comments about how I had a smart mouth and how I sounded like his ex. I was adamantly denied that, and it would further inflame our arguments. I would say, "Allen, I am not putting you down or calling you names." He would then respond, "But you got a smart mouth." That honestly confused me at first. Our disagreements went on to become more frequent, and the insults would still follow. There were even times my mother would have conversations with Allen, and he would get defensive really quickly and then strike back abrasively.

This behavior went on for almost two years of our marriage before I could pinpoint the reason he seemed to become so combative with women. What the heck was going on? Until God gave me insight, I was wondering how long we could stay married like this. However, it was after an altercation that involved Allen and another woman that God allowed me to see beyond his anger. I was present for this one. Allen had a musical project that he was working on with a client which was a woman.

Some words were exchanged, and then the conversation escalated. The woman began making sharp comments while being borderline rude, but before I could jump in, Allen abruptly pulled me to the side and said I can't deal with disrespectful women. Then he took those comments to another level. This is why men call women out their names! I said, "Hold on. I know she was not all the way right, but you can't let her get you to this point." Then he said it. This is what makes me not like women; their mouths. It was like a light bulb went off!

I sat him down a few weeks after that and said, "Babe, why don't you like women?" He responded, "I do." I replied, "No, you don't." Al responded, "What makes you think that?"

My wife began to share with me the anger I would demonstrate when it came to talking to women. Especially when a woman would pull one of my triggers like having an elevated tone, saying what I felt were mean comments, or anytime I felt any threat of emasculation.

I began to ponder, and it began to make a lot of sense. It not only explained why I went off on the woman in my wife's story but also why I would go off so hard on her. As much as I wanted to deny it, my heart was bearing witness to this revelation. My wife even pointed out how I was not aggressive with men even when in heated situations. I began to replay the memories and experiences of my past with my ex-wives of embarrassment. I could feel the disgust rising. Those non-acknowledged feelings and encounters were instrumental in creating hateful thoughts towards women, all because how I was mistreated – *"It was time for freedom." Quiet as it was kept, I could not even make love to my Jay because I could not adequately love her without remembering the pain.* As

I said, it was a problem I did not see coming from my addiction to porn, masturbation, and abuse.

My wife and I worked through my hate of women head-on. I had to allow myself to learn from her without feeling inferior. I began to learn how to have arguments with her without being abrasive or insulting. More importantly, I had to ask God to help me understand, respect, and love women again. Because nine times out of ten as a Pastor and Leader, my job is to help heal women, not destroy them or make them feel unsafe, demeaned, or to trigger past abuse. I refuse to be a man of God with no care for the women God entrusts me to be in my ministry.

BRINGING IT ALTOGETHER

Jesus stated in *Mark 7:11*, ***"For from within, out of the heart of men, proceed evil thoughts…"*** You all let me tell you; the thoughts of my heart weren't holy; THEY WERE MALICIOUS. Proverbs 4:23 recommends us to keep watch over our hearts because it holds our treasures, and in our hearts, has the potential for good or evil. Initially, the heart is full of wickedness - Jerimiah 17:9 says, but when it is purified, we will see and experience the presence of God - Matthew 5:8. With such potential within us, is it any wonder that we are encouraged to commit to persistence in protecting our heart?

So how do we remove the impurities and uncover those secrets of the heart spoken of in Psalms 44:21? The answer is through our Father (God The Creator). He knows what litters the landscape of our hearts. He tells us in Revelation 2:23 that ***"I am He who searches the minds and hearts"*** and again in *Hebrews 4:13* that ***"all things are open and laid bare"*** to His eyes.

Sometimes we may not know what inner sin lies within, but He does. When dealing with addictions, it is necessary to get to the root. The heart is the root.

Like David, we too can say, ***"Search me, O God, and know my heart ... and lead me in the everlasting way"*** Psalms 139:23-24. Then be ready for God to bring all things to the surface to be dealt with it. Put your hand over your heart and say, no more hiding ***come out! In Jesus' name!***

LET'S PRAY

I don't want to lead you in a word for word prayer. I want you to pray from your heart, mean it! Declare what you need and how you are going to change it. Remember, being truthful and transparent with yourself is what brings freedom to your life. Don't be embarrassed; it's just you and God. *You will overcome by the words out of your mouth, Revelation 12:11* – YOU GOT THIS, IN JESUS NAME

RECAP "YOUR HEART HAS THOUGHTS"

- What can hinder the purpose of your heart's purpose?
- Escalation of your addiction
- Problems you don't see coming
- Unforgiveness from the past
- Lack of love from past hurt

REFLECTION

What does God want to get out of your heart that has been hiding there due to your addiction?

Journal

_____

_____

_____

_____

_____

_____

_____

_____

_____

_____

_____

_____

_____

The Eye Gate

"Hell and decay are never satisfied, and a person's eyes are never satisfied."
Proverbs 27:20 (Gods Word Translation)

By the time I hit my 30's, porn had me so bound that I had stayed in adult theaters for hours upon hours. After wearing myself out from the euphoria of indulging myself, I would be so drained I would fall asleep right in the theater where there were others like me. There were even times I would get approached by others to share their experience with them. That was an easy no because my experiences were only for me. My eyes witnessed so much they never closed. I saw things no one should witness. Which once again opened my eye gate even wider. Being in the theater allowed me to witness other couples to come in and do what they enjoyed, which caused voyeurism to plant its desires in me. Accepting the invitations of other couples began to be extended, and although enticed, I would say no because contracting an STD was not an option for me. Safe sex was an afterthought in those types of places.

But what I did contract was another type of STD, "Sexual Transmitted Demons." Voyeurism became yet another fetish that I brought into my marriages, what I experienced in those theaters I wanted to encounter within my marriages. I had to have that same excitement. And as I tried to explore this behavior within my ex-wives, their repulsion to my request pushed me deeper into the acceptance of porn, voyeurism, my fetishes, and masturbation had provided me.

The scripture you read as you began this chapter gave a very eye-opening comparison of **hell and decay** related to **a person's eyes,** which must be explored. The scripture said that hell, decay, and **our** (you and I) eyes are **never satisfied**. The word **never** implies that the opposite of what **never** is referring to won't change. It will always be that way. Think about that, never! This means that because of this unchanging truth, we must learn how to guard what you and I allow into our eye gate, and what our eye gate desires to look upon. *What enters through the eye gate won't lock the gate behind it.*

The lack of satisfaction Proverbs 27:20 is talking about is due to one of the most significant issues you and I will face regarding the eye, which is lust. Lust is defined as a strong desire, usually for sex, but can also apply to other tangible items in our lives. Lust is never satisfied due to it having no limitation or fence in how it operates. When lust is in operation, it cannot restrict, nor will it keep boundaries. However, desire has been known to start small and grow. And it won't stop growing until you cut its head off, or dig up its root. A dug-up root can't grow due to it any longer being attached to the life source. Again, we must be careful about what we feast upon with our eyesight, along with what we extend our affectionate attention to because the opportunity to lust will always be present because we are equipped with sight!

HELPING THE EYES

So how do you and I deal with lust since our sight is not going anywhere? We must help the eyes by monitoring what enters its gate. Next, we must start with crucifying our desire to indulge in the addiction we are tied to by nailing it to the cross **on a daily basis**! You have to remember every day that **"nothing good dwells in us, that is, in our flesh" - Romans 7:18**. Our fleshly addictions will never desire boundaries or tell you and me, "Enough."

So know when we follow the Holy Spirit's direction, we can die to our flesh, which means we are dying only to what is without remorse destroying us, **"sexual immorality, impurity, passion, evil desire, and covetousness" - Colossians 3:5**. All we are dying to is death's existence in our lives. That kind of death is worth dying every day for– 1 Corinthians 15:31. For in such dying, we choose life – Deuteronomy 30:19. You may be asking, what does that look like? Well, start by bringing Jesus and the craving face to face. Yes, face to face. Meaning, begin to talk to God about what you are feeling. Remove the secret(s) and start an honest dialogue with God. God, you know what I'm dealing with, you know what I like, you see how much I am attracted to this addiction "impurity" (say what you like, it's ok). Help me with what I desire, what I crave, what I thirst for daily. What do I need to do to be free? Are you even ready to be free? Explore that too! Just be honest with God. DON'T BE ASHAMED!! Don't be embarrassed to talk to your Father.

And know whenever you are really ready to deal with you, your lust will awaken, and you must be willing to look it in its eye! In other words, CONFRONT IT! Stand flat-footed and deal with your impure desires. Those unclean desires are used to giving you **the feeling associated with what you want**. But when you decide to deal with the feeling, you must demand **the want** to tell you **why** you want it. That gives you a chance to deal with the lust logically and not just through sensation. This allows you to "Annihilate It!"

Confrontation is a vital component of annihilating anything. It's not many people's favorite thing, but it has the potential to invoke freedom. We often, unfortunately, go to great lengths to avoid confrontation. I was one of those. However, after becoming a leader, I learned in order to be effective, confrontation was necessary. The issues of a community require face to face attention. And with a leadership assignment upon my life, I had no choice but to face my impurities because they were keeping me from a fulfilling relationship with God, quality earthly relationships, and the promises of God.
Confrontation = Annihilation:

- Admit You Like What You Like. You Have To Confront
- Confront The Why. "Why Do You Like It"
- Ask, Does God Accept What I'm Liking, Would It Be Allowed In The Kingdom of God or Heaven?

The moment you stop liking something or someone is the moment, the nirvana, excitement, and desire can begin to subside. ***Anything you don't like, you won't desire.*** Listen, I don't like pain, so I don't put myself in any situation that will cause me to experience pain. I hate roaches, so I keep anywhere I abide clean. Get my point?

LET'S PRAY

I don't want to lead you in a word for word prayer. I want you to pray from your heart, mean it! Declare what you need and how you are going to change it. Remember, being truthful and transparent with yourself is what brings freedom to your life. Don't be embarrassed; it's just you and God. You will overcome by the words out of your mouth, Revelation 12:11 – YOU GOT THIS, IN JESUS NAME.

RECAP "THE EYE GATE"

What is it going to take to be able to focus on what God desires for you?

Confrontation = Annihilation:

- Admit You Like What You Like. You Have To Confront

- Confront The Why. "Why Do You Like It"

- Ask, Does God Accept What I'm Liking, Would It Be Allowed In The Kingdom of God "Heaven"

REFLECTION

How will you make sure what enters your eye gates will give you peace?

Journal

_____

_____

_____

_____

_____

_____

_____

_____

_____

_____

_____

_____

_____

_____

I Was Yoked Before I Was Hitched

I gave her permission, and it cost me 40 years of my life. I gave her rights to me, everything, and everyone connected to me.
-Allen K. Hunter

This portion of the devotional will take the discussion of guilty hands, the eye gate, and thoughts in the heart to another level spiritually. Initially, when deeper spiritual truths are exposed, fear tends to surface. However, I do not want that to happen here. The goal is for you to know what drives the desires you and I battle in regard to remaining pure in our lifestyle. A sexually impure lifestyle opens one up to spiritual attachments. And there are two spirits we must discuss, which both equally deal with the man or woman when granted access. They utilize the gender of the human host and pervert the desire of the host from that point.

Have you ever heard of Incubus (male demon) and Succubus (female demon), also known as "Spirit Husband or Spirit Wife,"? This is not a common dialogue being held in the church, but definitely should be. All through the Bible, the word speaks of unclean spirits. Unclean spirits in the Bible were known as spirits that influenced sexual immorality reference Jude 1:6-7, sickness as referenced in Acts 8:7, and infirmities as referenced in Luke 8:2. These examples are just some of what the Bible explains as unclean spirits known as demons and wicked spirits.

"I battled with the unclean spirit of Succubus for many years and didn't even realize that I was yoked before I was hitched!" I was literally married to the Spirit Wife, known as Succubus, legally in the spirit. At the time, I did not realize that there are natural legal rights we possess on earth and spiritual legal rights that exist in the spiritual realm. And our activity on Earth determines what in the spiritual realm has legal rights to function, influence, and oppress. As I previously stated, for over four decades, while not being aware, I was in a marriage in which I was legally very obligated to. Now that was quite a statement! Please see the key terms to know below so you will be able to follow along easier.

Incubus: an evil male demon of the night that lays on you as you sleep. This demon or spirit has sexual intercourse mostly with a woman while she is asleep during the night or day, and moves on to the next victim.

Succubus: an evil female demon of the night that lays on you as you sleep. This demon or spirit has sexual intercourse mostly with a man while he is asleep during the night or day, and moves on to the next victim.

Spirit Husband: particularly pursues a spiritual relationship with the woman, forming a powerful life-long bond with her that often results in the birth of spiritual children.

Spirit Wife: particularly pursues a spiritual relationship with the man, forming a powerful life-long bond with him that often results in the birth of spiritual children.

In the previous paragraph, I mentioned "married," let's talk about this for a brief moment. The words m*arried and hitched,* Word Hippo defines as *united by a common aim or common characteristic.* Common is defined as mutual or alike. Succubus and I had been acquainted since I was a child. The door was opened when Peter first opened his mouth. Succubus came in the door while at the same time, entering my imagination. Then once my first act of masturbation took place, spiritually Succubus and I became one. Intimacy had been established.

Many people today don't believe in the reality of the spiritual realm. The belief in the existence of spiritual beings can be difficult because we are so accustomed to this physical realm where senses like sight, smell, taste, hearing, and touching defines reality. However, the word of God validates that there are an authentic spiritual realm in and spirits that dwell within it - *When an evil spirit comes out of a person, it goes through dry places looking for a place to rest. But it doesn't find any. Then it says, 'I'll go back to the home I left – Luke 11:24 (GW)*. Due to the lack of awareness of spiritual teaching in the body of Christ, many can only speculate the truth of supernatural beings, therefore lacking vital information. However, we cannot afford to lack the knowledge of the spiritual realm anymore, *as the Bible says in Hosea, "my people are destroyed from the lack of knowledge..."*. We have a real enemy we are facing. *The key to defeating your enemy is to understand them. Understand their ways and nature. Then you can discover their weakness and be able to defeat them.*

Let me offer one more term people have rarely or ever heard of is *"demons of the night."* This is another term for Incubus and Succubus. The label "demons of the night" is also where they get the word nightmare from due to them primarily attacking at night. The term is essential for you to know. You must get this point also, the two demons that you *now* know about as Incubus and Succubus's other primary objective and activity is to have spiritual, *casual sex* with multiple people when they team up to function as one. It is exactly what we know as a threesome but in the spirit. When Incubus and Succubus team-up, these demons have also been known to latch on to one particular person, forming a powerful lifelong bond unseen, creating what is likened to as a marriage (a secret marriage).

People encounter Incubus and Succubus during impure sexual acts as they sleep. Many people experience "wet dreams" or even the sensation of *"having actual sex"* when they awake from a dream. This is the work of Incubus and Succubus. I often refer to these two unclean spirits, "STD" Sexual Transmitted Demons.

WOMEN, THIS IS FOR YOU!

Let us talk about "Spirit Children." Spirit Children are a deep mysterious experience and **are like** actual physical children. Spirit Children come into existence through the order of the spiritual husband to steal and cause confusion in the life of a woman. They are the offspring of the Spirit Husband.

Spirit Children are spiritually responsible for hindering many women's marriages unknown to them. And if a woman that is in union with the Spirit Husband manages to get married, it will cause problems. It is challenging to believe, but there is so much that occurs within this earthly realm in which there is no explanation. Sometimes a woman's issues are spiritual and not earthly. As I previously stated, the church isn't aware enough of the operations of the spiritual realm to have insight into these matters.

The Spirit Husband is so possessive of the women who have been yoked to him on the verge of marriage; he will begin to launch attacks (Spirit Children) against that human woman from the spirit realm. Remember, the yoking came through the living of an impure lifestyle by way of impure activities. For the Spirit Husband, the earthly man is real competition. Why? Because the Spirit Husband wants to be the only one to satisfy his wives. The Spirit Husband will summon the Spirit Children to attack the woman by arousing the woman. The woman will come into contact with a breast sucking sensation in their dreams. It can also result in a full sexual encounter. *This can cause the woman to climax or orgasm in reality based on a real stimulation occurring in the spirit. Intimacy causes two to become one.* Encounters such as these with the Spirit Husband yields an outcome of spiritual marriage with the human woman. The Spirit Husband has also been known to prevent the woman he is yoked with from having earthly children because of *jealousy.*

Let me give you some more information about the activities of the Spirit Children and how they deal with human women from the spiritual realm. You must know what their activity looks like, along with the various ways one can experience them. Remember, if you have the following occurrences listed below, coupled with real sensations, the involvement of real feelings, and the difficult tasks or separating the dream encounter from the waking world you are living in, it is an indication that you are coming up against a spiritual tie.

- Dreaming of kissing a person
- Having sex in your dream
- Playing with children in your dream
- Nursing/breastfeeding a child in your dream
- Taking a child in your dream
- Losing your pregnancy in your dream
- Masturbating in your dream
- Having an affair with an unknown or known person in your dream

Listen, this list could get much longer. And let us remember all this can manifest from participation in impure activities, secretive or otherwise. You are probably thinking, "All this in a devotional, jumping jellybeans! Yes ma'am, all of this in a devotional.

MORE INSIGHT

The Spirit Husband or Wife does not tolerate opponents of any kind in the life of the person they are bound to and will go to the extreme to get rid of the competition. *As stated before, these demons are jealous!* I was attached to Succubus for years and never knew what I was dealing with until one day, the Holy Spirit sat me down and showed me what was happening. Once I began to learn about my enemy with how she operated, I began to understand all the hell I was experiencing with my former marriages! Having been married o*ne, two, three times, and now on my fourth and final marriage in Jesus' name, I know a thing or two about spiritual opposition!*

With the insight I shared with you in this devotional, I was able to defeat her, Succubus. But before then, she had me doing things I should have known better not to do. But spiritual oppression and possession are not rational. It deals only with your intellect to carry out the strategic instruction while using your body *(the place where your spirit dwells)* to adhere itself to while having a voice to fuel your impure desires.

I was once mindlessly masturbating in public places like the bathroom of the church, in my car, and deceitfully running up various friends' cable bills renting pornographic movies. I would feel convicted in one moment throwing out all the pornographic movies I had, and then upon the next urge, running to my apartment's dumpster to get the pornographic items back out! Not to mention I was doing all of this while playing the drums in church and preaching!

Close Your Mouth! Trust me; She, Succubus, wasn't going away easy! Don't underestimate demons and evil spirits; they will have you doing crazy things to feed that fleshly appetite for the impure things you enjoy! Remember, you have got to be honest with yourself; you have probably done some crazy things to experience your form of sexual pleasure. *KEEP IT 100 WITH YOURSELF!*

It took and takes consistent confrontation, prayer, fasting, rejecting Succubus/Incubus, and seeking strategies from God! Hey You, the time is coming where you're going to have to refuse what isn't healthy for your spirit; THERE'S POWER IN A NO! I finally got a spiritual divorce. I will never forget how it went down, and I remember as if it was yesterday. I was sitting in my office at work around 3:17 am. I was preparing and studying for our ministry's Bible study when God put me asleep, and I began to dream. I began to hear a female voice saying, *"You don't want me here anymore! You don't like me!"* As I looked up to see who was talking to me, I witnessed a black female silhouette gathering her purse saying, *"I'm leaving, I'm not welcomed here anymore, and I'm leaving."* As she continued to talk, she walked towards the front door with her purse, saying, *"You hurt me."* As I tried to face her, she immediately stormed out the front of the house, saying, *"I'm Gone!"* slamming the door behind her. At that moment, I felt a physical weight lift from me! I had a spiritual dream, which resulted in a physical release. I awoke and immediately began to thank the Lord! I then heard, *"You Are Free Now!"*

Noticed I said one, **"she was in my house**, two she stated, **"I didn't want or like her any longer,"** and three, **"you hurt me."**

I was the one who opened the door and welcomed her into my house. At the age of 5, not having a clue, I opened the door. As time went on, I had the ability to give a yes or no soundly; as permission was granted with each impure act, Succubus was able to walk through the door and throughout my life, making herself at home. I gave her permission, and it cost me 40 years of my life. I gave her rights to me, everything, and everyone connected to me. But at the time, I didn't realize it. I am writing this devotional so that now you can know it! You currently have the knowledge and the power to make a change with God's help!

Real quick note: Remember Succubus telling me, "I Hurt Her." Know this, Demons and Spirits are emotional, Like us, they have complex personalities, read Luke 8:28

Finally, I want you to be aware of how these spirits enter our lives. The Spirit Husband/Wife or Incubus/Succubus will enter your house/temple by way of:

- Fornication
- Masturbation
- Pornography
- Carnality
- Bitterness & Unforgiveness
- Fear & Doubt
- Witchcraft
- Abuse
- Molestation
- Emotional Wounds/ Trauma
- Soul Ties
- Fantasy
- Spiritual Warfare

The door is open, in which they will walk right on in, slam the door, and lock it! They can enter your house/temple when impurities of every kind drive the activities.

LET'S PRAY

I don't want to lead you in a word for word prayer. I want you to pray from your heart, mean it! Declare what you need and how you are going to change it. Remember, being truthful and transparent with yourself is what brings freedom to your life. Don't be embarrassed; it's just you and God. *You will overcome by the words out of your mouth, Revelation 12:11* – YOU GOT THIS, IN JESUS NAME

RECAP "I WAS YOKED BEFORE I WAS HITCHED"

How do the unclean spirits of Incubus, Succubus, and others enter our lives?

- Fornication
- Masturbation
- Pornography
- Carnality
- Bitterness & Unforgiveness
- Fear & Doubt
- Witchcraft
- Abuse
- Molestation
- Emotional Wounds/ Trauma
- Soul Ties
- Fantasy
- Spiritual Warfare

REFLECTION

What steps are you going to take to begin to stop the activities of unclean spirits in your life?

Journal

_____

_____

_____

_____

_____

_____

_____

_____

_____

_____

_____

_____

_____

_____

Confession is Good?

Confessions don't influence God to forgive us;
They can't bribe him.
-Allen K. Hunter

"IT'S *NECESSARY TO ADMIT YOU LIKE IT!"*
There are times we confess our sins for the sake of guilty
emotions, and not because we sincerely realize that our sin is a
problem. It's necessary, to be honest, that you like "*it,"your*
sin, that is, so much that you find yourself looking for that
particular experience continuously. The weight of any previous
guilt you felt disappearing as the drive for your acquired sin
ranges. If we would all be brutally honest, we could admit how
we ask for forgiveness in one breath and knew in our hearts
that the confession was not about stopping the sin, it was about
the release of guilt. Our sincerity lacked commitment; therefore, we would return to our vomit. I returned to my vomit for
many years.

> **Proverbs 26:11 (NCV)** *A fool who repeats his foolishness is*
> *like a dog that goes back to what it has thrown up.*

We have got to stop lying to ourselves because you must
know - *Transparency Will Save Your Soul.* We've all heard
the proverb, "confession is good for the soul." How many

confessions? My answer, "As much as your ego can stand and as much as your spirit says release." Admission will only be as authentic as your ego and pride will allow. God knows the hairs that are numbered on your head. God knows your answer before you speak it. God knows your weakness before you do. So, why only confess in part while hiding the whole truth? It truly only does you a great disservice.

The reason for transparency is one, accountability - your sin must be taken to the cross every day so you can receive freedom from guilt and condemning thoughts. Two, by admitting them to others, is another way of finding relief. By no longer imagining to be what we are not, we permit our friends to see who and what we are. Real friends will gladly bear your burdens with you as you continue to seek God's grace and be honest about your struggles. Exposing myself to my closest friends felt so liberating! I knew no one could use anything I have disclosed in this devotional against me because I have told on myself! I beat the spirit of gossip and the shame the devil would love to hold over me to the punch! I have had times when I have revealed just some of this testimony to people, and they got embarrassed for me or had attempted to rebuke my openness! I kindly respect their compassion, but I do not need it! I am finally at peace! I am completely free! The confession of your sins can yield your peace.

The third reason why transparency is essential is the mortification (meaning embarrassment) of sin - I found out in delays in dealing with my sins, what no one else could see, but I was hurting me. Listen, we are called to put to death any sins that creep around in our lives, both the big and the small. But it's easy to get lazy in this area until we face the embarrassment confession threatens. Often confession is the push we need to start dealing with and killing those dear sins that we have been wallowing within. Maybe your sins are not yet affecting anyone but yourself. Perhaps they are shredding apart your marriage. Both are toxic, and coming clean with them before your friends or whomever you confide in is the first step in putting them to death. Trusty counsel and confidants are a necessity. Not everyone can handle your confessions, nor are they equipped. Be prayerful about your trusted sources with whom you confess.

Another reason why transparency is essential is obedience. The best and most important reason we have to be real with trusted counsel is that we are obeying our Savior by confessing our sins. Confession usually precedes repentance. This is often the beginning of the freeing process. As believers, confession is vital in our walk with Jesus.

> If we say, "We aren't sinful" we are deceiving ourselves, and the truth is not in us. 9 God is faithful and reliable. If we confess our sins, he forgives them and cleanses us from everything we've done wrong – **1 John 1:8-9 (Gods Word Translation)**

The Bible says, ***"we were born into sin,"*** therefore our flesh will naturally desire or can I say, connect with sin automatically. Please understand, you didn't have to teach you how to cuss or fornicate; most likely, you did it naturally, right? But you did have to train yourself, and some of us are still in training on how not to cuss or fornicate, along with other things. Give it some thought. Please understand. We all have sinned, and for some, we're still sinning, so lying is useless.

Every time you fake it, you're hurting YOU and the ones that are connected to you. When you lie to yourself, you're also lying to God. God sees everything you do; it's like He has an HD cam, God sees everything so clear that you do, nothing is hidden. God said, *"A liar cannot tarry in His sight"* why because He has evidence, the proof. You simply cannot hide from God. This is why John said in scripture, "If we confess, He'll forgive." By confessing, you acknowledge God sees and knows about your impure activities; he is omnipresent. So do not attempt to walk in the spirit of deception, as I said before, be honest with God. God desires for you to self-identify and admit you have an issue. By doing that, you're saying "I NEED HELP" you're crying out to the helper. You are now beginning to build a relationship with a strong and trusty foundation.

I stated when this portion of the devotional began, "IT'S *NECESSARY TO ADMIT YOU LIKE IT!"* You have got to. Because if you don't, the sin part of our desires will conquer us every time. You must face when you like and enjoy doing what you do. Acknowledge how it pleases you and satisfies your flesh when in prayer to God. And when you can do that, your relationship with God grows because there is no fluff in the way. Your heart clears up as your conscience clears up. As this happens, you will begin to ask yourself this question, "IS THIS WHAT GOD WANTS?" and "IS THIS DESIRE WORTH MY PEACE?". The *consequences of experiencing sin are the next thing to consider.*

LET'S DIG DEEPER IN CONFESSION

Here I want to officially define confession as the making known of something that was previously secret or unknown (WordHippo.com). Know **confession helps us to obtain grace, and** grace is not for everybody; it's only for the needy. Are you needy? **God resists the proud** but gives grace to the humble. God treats us with even more incredible kindness, just as the Scriptures say:

> *"God opposes everyone who is proud, but he blesses all who are humble with undeserved grace." – James 4:6*

To obtain God's grace, we must first acknowledge our need for HIS grace! **Acknowledge you need His help**." If we refuse to acknowledge our need, we won't receive his kindness, but His wrath. This point is often misplaced among those of us who broadcast grace. We've been taught that "we are as righteous, holy, and perfect as Jesus," and yes, that is right; in Christ, we're all those things. But we must be saved. We must have admitted we believe that Jesus is our Lord and Savior and that He died on the cross for our sin while accepting His authority is our lives.

But what if there is a separation between your identity and experience? Meaning, what if when an individual receives Jesus Christ, and He redefines our identity, the person fails to receive it truly. For example, *"I know I am righteous, but I don't* feel *righteous, I'm battling with unrighteous thoughts."* You've got two choices; You can act as if there's no problem, or you can come to God and ask Him to help you understand what He has gifted to you through Christ Jesus. The dominion of grace is available for us to receive grace in our time of need.

Confessions don't influence God to forgive us; They can't bribe him. One of the primary purposes of c**onfession is to break the power of sin**. Another objective of confession is awareness. God intended for confession to keep us aware of Him.

God intended for us to desire righteousness. We don't have to be taught to enjoy the pleasures of sin. It is a part of being born into our flesh, connected directly to our old sin nature. For righteousness to replace that nature, we must begin with exchanging desires. If you are wondering if a desire–exchange needs to take place, ask God to help you to become sensitive to guilt and the need to hide. The regret of an action thought, or behavior is another red flag that something is wrong and needs to be confronted! Confrontation, followed by some much necessary confession, is an excellent way to stand face to face with sin. The following scripture is a great one to meditate on frequently.

> *When I kept silent about my sins, my bones began to weaken because of my groaning all day long. 4 Day and night your hand laid heavily on me. My strength shriveled in the summer heat. Selah. 5 I made my sins known to you, and I did not cover up my guilt. I decided to confess them to you, O Lord. Then you forgave all my sins. Selah – **Psalms 32:3-5 (Gods Word Translation)***

People talk to me all the time that are wavering in their faith on account of some past or present sin(s). But at times, neglect wanting to tell me what the sin is. I can literally see their internal battle with shame and their desire to be free and at peace. Can you relate? Is this you? Why don't you drag that dark impure thing into the light! Talk to your heavenly Father or locate trusted counsel and confront sin through confession.

Please understand, sin thrives in darkness, and we are called to be children of the light, 1 Thessalonians 5:5. Note that ***David suffered because he "kept silent."*** Here's the equation: ***Sin + silence = suffering!*** This is the equation that leads so many of us to hide as suffering happens silently. But freedom is NOW! Right now! No more of the enemy holding your sin over your head, tormenting you and bullying you into loneliness and shame! Take God's hand now and start holding on tight!

Here is where you shout because you are being invited to work out the new equation Jesus afforded you to by dying on the cross: ***Sin + confession = healing*** Make this your common practice:

> *So, admit your sins to each other and pray for each other so that you will be healed. Prayers offered by those who have God's approval are effective – **James 5:16 (Gods Word Translation)***

As a church leader, James knew *(about admittance)*. He understood that one of the ways we receive God's grace is through our grace-giving brothers and sisters. James, in this scripture, was not trying to shackle you with an accountability partner; he was giving you a key for living free and whole. ***Confession acknowledges your need for* God's help!**

The enemy does not mind troubling your mind, locking up your joy, destroying your character, and breaking your communication with God. Satan is banking on your silence so he can do just that! Know that the silence of sin is utterly destructive; we must not be passive with condemning, tormenting silence!

LET'S PRAY

I don't want to lead you in a word for word prayer. I want you to pray from your heart, mean it! Declare what you need and how you are going to change it. Remember, being truthful and transparent with yourself is what brings freedom to your life. Don't be embarrassed; it's just you and God. *You will overcome by the words out of your mouth, Revelation 12:11* – YOU GOT THIS, IN JESUS NAME

RECAP "CONFESSION"

Why is confession so vital in fighting the bondage of sin and addiction?

- accountability
- confessing to others releases you from shame & guilt
- confession is requested of us by God
- we receive grace in confession

REFLECTION

What is your biggest fear about confessing your sin or addictions?

Journal

Repent, The Time Is Now!

Any time you stop liking something or someone, the relationship or connection you had with it is over.
-Allen K. Hunter

Someone presented this question to me, "Is repentance a change of mind or a turning from sin?*"* I replied, "Good Question, let's talk about it."

Why even ask this question? The answer lies in the definition. Repentance is defined as a transformation of mind, not turning away from sin. In Greek, "repentance" is *metanoia*, which means "a change of mind." In the church, we often speak of repentance as "a turning away from sin." There is a useful purpose for this; however, turning from sin happens after a change of mind occurs.

In scripture, repentance is often connected with the topic of salvation or the decision of asking for forgiveness, which it should be. Nevertheless, there is a need to ensure the repentance comes with the accompanying of what happens before that. The work of the Holy Spirit has a great deal to do with one getting to the point of repentance so that they can REPENT! This is called being in a repentant state.

What happens when the Holy Spirit initiates His work to bring a person to salvation? The Spirit gives the person dealing with sin, a personal understanding, and a sound conviction that

the sin in their life causes disconnection from Him and a life
free from bondage. The facts regarding their real spiritual con-
dition reveal themselves to help bring conscious awareness to
an individual. Then the Holy Spirit can further speak to the
heart of that individual's sin, the price Jesus paid for them, the
nature of Jesus that they can now have because He suffered on
the cross, and the need for faith in Jesus to save them from
their sin. From the convicting work of the Holy Spirit (John
16:8), the person repents; he or she changes their mind about
sin, the Savior, and salvation.

When a repentant person changes their mind about sin,
that transformation naturally leads to *a turning away from sin*.
Sin to a repentant individual has become no longer enjoyable,
desirable, or fulfilling. The act of sin itself has brought with it
weighty condemnation, also known as guilt *(I had many moments
of this)*. Liken, to someone in a relationship that is no longer in
love with their lover, when a repentant individual begins to dis-
like what they loved; they will move forward without looking
back. **Any time you stop liking something or someone, the
relationship or connection you had with it is over**. And because of that, a repentant individual begins to seek ways to cor-
rect their behavior - Luke 19:8 (NCV)

> But Zacchaeus stood and said to the Lord, "I will give half of
> my possessions to the poor. And if I have cheated anyone, I
> will pay back four times more."

So, eventually, the result of a change of mind about sin are
respectable actions. The individual turns away from sin toward
faith in the Savior, and that faith is shown in action – James
2:17 **In the same way, faith by itself is dead if it doesn't
cause you to do any good things.**

Here is another example that will bring the point home regarding being *repentant* versus *in repentance.* If a person is having an extramarital affair, they may "know" or "believe" the extramarital affair is morally wrong. However, genuine repentance that results in the change of mind would cause the adulterer to cut off the relationship, which is the *work* portion of the extramarital affair. The work is the action which is demonstrated in the behavior.

If a person wants to repent for real, they should not only mentally acknowledge that the affair is wrong but ask themselves, ``*What will I do differently?"* And the answer would need to yield different behavior along with different choices. A repentant person has remorse. Repentance is derived from that remorse. As John The Baptist said, "Produce fruit in keeping with repentance" - Luke 3:8.

The following scripture gives a great example of how our attitude should adjust when we learn right from wrong. John gave the people the following commands with some specific examples in Luke 3:10-14:

> *The crowds asked him, "What should we do?" He answered them, "Whoever has two shirts should share with the person who doesn't have any. Whoever has food should share it too."*
>
> *Some tax collectors came to be baptized. They asked him, "Teacher, what should we do?" He told them, "Don't collect more money than you are ordered to collect."*
>
> *Some soldiers asked him, "And what should we do?" He told them, "Be satisfied with your pay and never use threats or blackmail to get money from anyone."*

The point I'm making is when your mind has changed, so will your actions, aka "works"; therefore, one can bank that the repentance is sincere. Like most of you, I have repented so many times, going back and forth, feeling guilty, but the truth is back then, I never changed my imagination (thoughts); consequently, my actions never changed either. I kept sinning and indulging in impurity until I sat in a repentant posture, which triggered authentic repentance and caused me to change my thoughts (imagination) and my desires.

So, allow me to say this, repentance is a change of mind. In relationship to salvation, repentance is *a change of mind from an embrace of sin to rejection of sin and rejection of Christ to faith in Christ.* Such repentance is something only God can enable - Acts 11:18. True repentance does have the ability to result in a change of behavior instantly, but a change of behavior over time is better than nothing. Do not be too hard on yourself. Deliverance is a process of progression and learning.

LET'S PRAY

I don't want to lead you in a word for word prayer. I want you to pray from your heart, mean it! Declare what you need and how you are going to change it. Remember, being truthful and transparent with yourself is what brings freedom to your life. Don't be embarrassed; it's just you and God. *You will overcome by the words out of your mouth, Revelation 12:11* – YOU GOT THIS, IN JESUS NAME

RECAP "REPENT THE TIME IS NOW"

- Repentance is a change of mind.
- To be repentant is to experience remorse.

REFLECTION

What desires tend to draw you back in so that you find yourself going back on your decision to repent?

Journal

_____

_____

_____

_____

_____

_____

_____

_____

_____

_____

_____

_____

_____

Final Thoughts

He battled with his enemies successfully, but he unsuccessfully battled with himself.
-Allen K. Hunter

Through repentance *(revolving back to obey God's directions)*, we can regain power, as long as we are willing to follow God's organized path for us as people. God always shows His grace in the Believer's journey, so we should not run away from Him when we cave to the seduction to live impure lives. Instead, we can run to him for mercy and help. The only significant answers to spiritual problems are found in discipleship, godly obedience to the Word, and prayer.

> *For our high priest is able to understand our weaknesses. He was tempted in every way that we are, but he did not sin. 16 Let us, then, feel very sure that we can come before God's throne where there is grace. There we can receive mercy and grace to help us when we need it* **– Hebrews 4:15-16 (NCV)**

When we're born again, our spirit becomes renewed but not our physical body or the memory of the senses that were aroused. Our body can experience those feelings it had even after we accept Jesus. *The flesh can lust off of memory. This is why we have to submit this flesh to God every day.*

Samson was a man who was powerfully anointed and set apart for God's use even before he was born just like us. He was extraordinary with a strength that no other human had at that time. *But he could not tame the lust his flesh wanted*.

Let's look at this in detail; what *made Samson fall prey to sexual temptations?* It wasn't Delilah or how seductive she was. However, she seduced him pretty good. The root of Delilah being able to seduce had to do with Samson. Ponder for a moment. The inability for Samson to be able to discipline his body, his desire, and attention for a woman, Samson failed to handle his appetite for sex. This is just like some of us. *He battled with his enemies successfully, but he unsuccessfully battled with himself.*

Here's the aha moment; it was in what Delilah used to capture Samson. Delilah used his own vulnerabilities, weakness, tiredness, hormones, feelings, and sexuality. The ultimate battle we need to fight successfully is *self,* and we will undoubtedly need to fight this battle more than once. Listen, It's a daily battle. So, what can we do?

> *But clothe yourselves with the Lord Jesus Christ, and make no provision for [nor even think about gratifying] the flesh in regard to its improper desires – Romans 13:14 (AMP)*
>
> *⁵ So put to death and deprive of power the evil longings of your earthly body [with its sensual, self-centered instincts] immorality, impurity, sinful passion, evil desire, and greed, which is [a kind of] idolatry [because it replaces your devotion to God] – Colossians 3:5 (AMP)*

Allow me to leave you with this, have a funeral for your flesh daily, *do not indulge in the flesh, have thought substitutions prepared when impure cravings surface, make the decision not to gratify your lust by denying self and other things that stimulate you instead of God.* YOU CAN DO THIS, NOW ACCOMPLISH IT!

A Pastor Who Struggled, Now Strengthened
KINGDOM AUTHORITY | KINGDOM POWER

Allen K. Hunter

RECAP "FINAL THOUGHTS"

What will the enemy try to use against us during this process of deliverance?

- Our own vulnerabilities, weakness, tiredness, hormones, feelings, and sexuality.

FINAL REFLECTION

What will you do to strengthen your decision to leave your addictions and begin your healing process?

Journal

_____

_____

_____

_____

_____

_____

_____

_____

_____

_____

_____

_____

_____

_____

_____

Resources

I want to acknowledge this book as a source of inspiration.

Total Deliverance from Spirit Husband & Spirit Wife Incubus & Succubus Demons, Rev. Ezekiel King, 2019 Copyright

Kat IP Pty Ltd 2008. Word Hippo. Retrieved from https://www.wordhippo.com/

About the Author

Allen grew up in the church where his parents – Pastor D.E.C and Artricia Matthews – were shining examples of serving a congregation in a pastoral capacity. Although he didn't think pastoring was for him, he did feel drawn to it. Initially, he focused on his first loves – music and drumming.

Pursuing those early passions paid off. Many doors opened for Allen professionally as a drummer, and he toured with legendary artists such as Mos Def, Black Eyed Peas, and Gil-Scott Heron, Source of Labor, The Washington State Mass, LaShaun Pace Rhodes, Tremayne Hawkins – among others.

Relocating to Houston, TX, he fine-tuned his music production skills under the production name "Aflat Muziq" for some of the music industry's biggest names – H-Town, JO-DECI, Silk, CeCe Peniston, Smokey Robinson, Lady Jay TMP, Sariyah of Empire, Chris Brown, Day 26, LINK, Bone Thug & Harmony, Lil' Flip, K-CI & JoJo, and Kathy Burrell.

Despite all of his professional success, Allen's personal struggles with porn addiction, rejection, depression, and low self-esteem that brought him to the feet of God, this is when Allen finally accepted his calling to be a minister/pastor.

Allen Hunter was officially ordained to minister in 2011 and pastoral leadership in 2012 under Apostle J.K. Sayles. The call on his life was clear. Allen had been chosen to preach the gospel of Jesus Christ. God's call is all he wants to do now. Pastor Allen's heart is for men to be repaired, restored, and effective in their lives and the lives of those around them.

He desires for our youth need to be healed and for God's people to overcome what has before been deemed as impossible. Without a doubt, Pastor Allen is called to the nations.

The strategy God has given to Pastor Allen is one he is sure to follow while making sure his own life-lines up with what he teaches and preaches. As he says, *"If y'all got to live right, so do I."*

Pastor Allen is now a published Author under Za'Van Gail Publishing and has released his first book entitled "PURE: Re-assigning the Purpose of Your Eyes, Heart, and Hands" a Holy Spirit lead devotional. This book is aimed at helping God's people to live a pure life.

ASKING FOR GOD'S HELP

"If you're like me, you often find yourself asking for God's help in making decisions. You might ask Him whether or not you should buy a new house, take a different job, or move to a new city. We want insider information so that we can know what God knows.

Of course, there is nothing wrong with wanting to make wise decisions, but instead of us just wanting to know what He knows, God would rather we want to get to know Him."

KINGDOM AUTHORITY | KINGDOM POWER

Allen K. Hunter

Social Media

Facebook AllenKHunter

Intagram @AllenKHunter

PastorAllen@DominionAndPowerMinistries.com

www.AllenKHunter.com

www.ingramcontent.com/pod-product-compliance
Lightning Source LLC
Chambersburg PA
CBHW071631040426
42452CB00009B/1580